MW01193650

ABOUT THE AUTHOR

Barb Asselin is a college professor and best-selling author who has published books in many different genres including education, cooking, law, real estate, internet marketing, entrepreneurship, baby sign language, fitness, office administration, children's fiction and children's non-fiction.

Barb has been fascinated, okay obsessed, with the Titanic since she first found a book on the Titanic in her parents' book collection when she was in middle school. She has seen all of the movies made regarding the Titanic and has researched it endlessly.

She loves to teach through her courses, books, and textbooks, and strives to make a connection with each student and reader. Barb lives in Canada with her husband, Mike, and two adorable daughters, Casey and Jamie. They enjoy music, skiing, golfing, running, and mixed martial arts.

COPYRIGHT INFORMATION

WHY YOU SHOULD READ THIS BOOK

Are you fascinated with the Titanic?

Have you wondered what it must have been like to work in those hot boiler rooms, or as a maid to a First Class passenger?

Have you wondered what it would have been like if you actually were a First Class passenger?

Did you watch James Cameron's Titanic and think, "How would I have survived the sinking?"

Well, this book is for you. Inside, you will find over 200 facts about the Titanic. There are facts about:

- Building the Titanic
- Crew of the Titanic
- Passengers of the Titanic
- Interior of the Titanic
- Maiden voyage of the Titanic
- Sinking of the Titanic
- Survivors of the Titanic
- Museums of the Titanic
- Movies about the Titanic
- Titanic's legacy

Ready? Let's go back to Titanic...

TITANIC FACTS:
200+ FACTS ABOUT THE UNSINKABLE SHIP

INTRODUCTION

Titanic is a word from Greek mythology meaning gigantic. At the time she was built, Titanic was the largest ship in existence.

Titanic was built because of competition. Cunard, a ship building company, launched the two fastest passenger ships in the world in 1907. They were the Mauritania and the Lusitania. The White Star Line, Cunard's rival ship building company, wanted to outdo these two new ships. Instead of focusing on speed, White Star Line would focus on luxury.

The White Star Line created the Olympic class passenger ship. It hired Harland & Wolff, its favored shipbuilder to build the Olympic class ships. It also

7

hired naval architect, Thomas Andrews, to design the ships. White Star Line started building the Olympic in 1908 and started building the Titanic in 1909.

It took over three years to build the great ship and less than three hours to sink it.

CHAPTER 1: BUILDING THE TITANIC

Sea trials of the Titanic on April 2, 1912

The RMS Titanic was built in Belfast, Ireland by the Harland and Wolff shipyard.

Thomas Andrews was the naval architect for the Titanic.

Work started on the Titanic on March 31, 1909 in yard number 401 at the shipyard.

Titanic was first launched in water on May 31, 1911.

Work was completed on Titanic on April 2, 1912.

Titanic was in service for only 5 days, from April 10, 1912 to April 15, 1912.

Titanic was an Olympic-Class Ocean Liner owned by the White Star Line.

Titanic was the sister ship of the Olympic, another Ocean Liner owned by the White Star Line.

She was 269m (882' 6") in length.

She was 53.3m (175') in height, from the keel to the top of the funnels.

Titanic had one 4-blade center propeller and two 3-blade wing propellers.

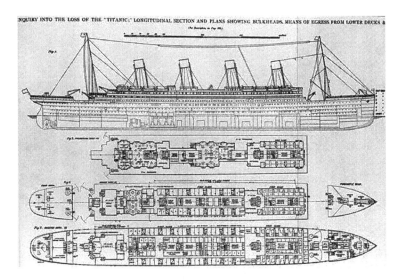

Plans for building the Titanic

Titanic's propellers were powered by two reciprocating steam engines.

Titanic's steam engines were fueled by 24 double-ended boilers and 5 single-ended boilers.

Titanic's cruising speed was 39 km/h (24 mph).

The Titanic only carried enough lifeboats for 1,178 people, just more than half of the passengers on her maiden voyage.

Titanic's top speed was 44 km/h (28 mph).

Approximately 3,000 men were hired to construct Titanic.

There were 3,000,000 rivets used in the construction of the hull of the Titanic.

The average worker received a weekly wage of £2 for working on the Titanic.

Almost 250 workers were injured during the construction of the ship.

Two workers died in construction accidents during building and fitting.

Six more workers died on board the ship.

The ship was considered by many to be unsinkable because it was built with sixteen lower compartments that were separated by watertight bulkheads. It was believed that even if two middle or four front compartments were breached, the ship could still float. Unfortunately, during its collision with the iceberg, five compartments were breached, causing it to sink.

Titanic (right) and her sister ship, the Olympic, in one of the only photographs of the two ships together

CHAPTER 2: CREW OF THE TITANIC

OFFICERS

This ship's captain was Commander Edward John Smith, RNR (Royal Naval Reserve). Captain Smith was 62 years of age when he perished on board Titanic.

Captain Smith

The Chief Officer of the Titanic was Lieutenant Henry Tingle Wilde, RNR. He was 39 years of age when he perished on board the Titanic.

The First Officer of the Titanic was Lieutenant William McMaster Murdoch, RNR. He was 39 years of age when he perished on board the Titanic.

The Second Officer of the Titanic was Sub-Lieutenant Charles Herbert Lightoller, RNR. He was 38 years of age and survived the sinking of the Titanic in Lifeboat B.

The Third Officer of the Titanic was Mr. Herbert John Pitman. He was 34 years of age and survived the sinking of the Titanic in Lifeboat 5.

The Fourth Officer of the Titanic was Sub-Lieutenant Joseph Groves Boxhall, RNR. He was 28 years of age and survived the sinking of the Titanic in Lifeboat 2.

The Fifth Officer of the Titanic was Sub-Lieutenant Harold Godfrey Lowe, RNR. He was 29 years of age and survived the sinking of the Titanic in Lifeboat 14.

The Sixth Officer of the Titanic was Mr. James Paul Moody. He was 24 years of age when he perished on board the Titanic.

DECK CREW

The Able Officer, or Boatswain, was in charge of all of the un-licensed deck crew.

The Able Officer assisted architect, Thomas Andrews, in his daily ship inspections.

There were 29 Able Bodied Seamen on board Titanic, each of whom was assigned to a lifeboat if there were no officers present.

There were two Boatswain Mates on board Titanic. They were in charge of the deck lines, cranes, winches, and lifeboat davits on the deck of the ship.

There were two Masters-at-Arms on Titanic. The Masters-at-Arms and the Chief Officer had the only keys to the firearms cabinet on board.

All seven quartermasters on board the Titanic survived the sinking. Their duties included steering the ship, managing signal flags, standing watch, and assisting with general navigation.

All six lookouts on board also survived the sinking. Their duty was to work two-man, two-hour shifts in the crow's nest. The crow's nest should have been equipped with binoculars, however, on Titanic's maiden voyage, the binoculars were locked away, and the key to unlock them was not on board.

ENGINEERING CREW

The engineers aboard the Titanic were the highest paid members of the crew.

There were 25 engineers and 10 electricians and boilermakers on board.

All of the engineers, electricians, and boilermakers were lost during the sinking.

Before the ship went down, they all stayed below decks to keep the pumps working and the generators working and the power on. Their actions were thought to delay the sinking by over an hour, allowing most of the lifeboats to launch.

There were 13 leading firemen and 163 firemen on the Titanic, who serviced 29 boilers and 159 furnaces.

Each fireman was in charge of one boiler and three furnaces.

Three leading firemen and 45 firemen survived the sinking.

There were 73 coal trimmers on the Titanic. Their job was to shovel coal from the coal bunkers down the coal chute to be shoveled by the firemen into the furnaces.

Approximately 20 coal trimmers survived the sinking.

There were 33 greasers employed on the Titanic. Their job was to ensure that all of the mechanical equipment on the ship was greased and lubricated.

Four greasers survived the sinking.

VICTUALLING CREW

There were 421 men and women on the Victualling Crew. 322 of these were stewards who worked in the dining saloons, public rooms, cabins, and recreational facilities for the various classes on board.

Approximately 60 stewards survived the sinking.

First Class Bedroom Stewards were responsible for three to five rooms each. Second Class Bedroom Stewards were responsible for 10 rooms each, and Third Class Stewards were responsible for approximately 25 rooms each.

The stewards in charge of the public toilets on board were called the Glory-Hole Stewards.

There were 23 female crew members on board. Of these 23, 20 were stewardesses, two were cashiers, and one was the "matron" of the ship. 20 of them survived the sinking.

62 members of the Victualling Crew worked in the galley and the kitchen as chefs, cooks, bakers, butchers, and scullions (dishwashers). Approximately 13 of these crew members survived.

RESTAURANT STAFF

There was a restaurant called *à la Carte*, located on B Deck. This restaurant was not operated by the White Star Line, but owned and operated by A.P. Luigi Gatti.

The *à la Carte* Restaurant carried a staff of 66 cooks, waiters, cleanup crew, and other crew. Only three survived the sinking, one male clerk and two female cashiers.

POSTAL CREW

The Titanic had five postal clerks who were in charge of processing all incoming and outgoing mail on the ship.

All five postal clerks perished during the disaster.

GUARANTEE GROUP

There were nine members of the Guarantee Group. Although they were considered part of the crew, they were given accommodation on the ship as passengers.

Their duties were to take the maiden voyage of the ship and oversee any work that was left to be done, or to fix any issues that arose during the voyage.

The group was supervised and headed by architect, Thomas Andrews.

All nine members of the Guarantee Group perished during the disaster.

SHIP'S ORCHESTRA

There were eight members of the orchestra.

All eight members travelled as second-class passengers aboard the ship.

None of the eight members survived the disaster.

Bandmaster and Violinist Wallace Hartley was 33 years of age when he perished during the sinking.

Pianist Theodore Ronald Brailey was 24 years of age when he perished during the sinking.

Cellist Rober Marie Bricoux was 20 years of age when he perished during the sinking.

Bassist John Frederick Preston Clark was 30 years of age when he perished during the sinking.

Violinist John Law Hume was 21 years of age when he perished during the sinking.

Violinist Georges Alexandre Krins was 23 years of age when he perished during the sinking.

Cellist Percy Cornelius Taylor was 32 years of age when he perished during the sinking.

Cellist John Wesley Woodward was also 32 years of age when he perished during the sinking.

Ship's Orchestra

CHAPTER 3: PASSENGERS OF THE TITANIC

Multimillionaire John Jacob Astor IV and his wife, Madeleine

On her maiden voyage, the Titanic carried 2,224 souls, consisting of both passengers and crew.

There were three classes of passengers on board: First Class, Second Class, and Third Class.

First Class passengers were the wealthiest on board and were businessmen, politicians, high-ranking military personnel, industrialists, bankers, and athletes.

A First Class ticket for one person aboard the Titanic cost between £30 (for a single berth) and £870 (for a parlour suite and personal promenade deck), which is the equivalent of approximately £2,515 and £71,778.

Many First class passengers traveled with staff members, such as valets, maids, children's nannies, chauffeurs, and cooking staff.

Many members of British aristocracy were on board, such as:

Lady Noel Leslie, the Countess of Rothes

Lady Noel Leslie

Sir Cosmo Duff-Gordon and his wife, Lady Lucy Duff-Gordon

Colonel Archibald Gracie IV

American socialites were also on board, such as:

Colonel John Jacob Astor IV and his wife, Madeleine

Millionaire Benjamin Guggenheim

US House of Representatives member, Isidor Straus and his wife, Ida

Pensylvania Railroad vice president John Thayer and his wife, Marian

Women's rights activist, Margaret Brown

Tennis star, Karl Behr

Silent film actress, Dorothy Gibson

US President Taft's military aide, Major Archibald Butt

Mrs. Charlotte Collyer and her daughter, Marjorie

Second Class passengers were middle class citizens and were comprised of teachers, authors, clergymen, and tourists.

The average ticket price for a Second Class passenger was £13, which would be approximately £1,090 today.

There were two Roman Catholic Priests on board who held Mass every day for the Second Class and Third Class passengers. Mass was held in English, Irish, French, German, and Hungarian.

Teacher Lawrence Beesley was aboard the ship and survived the sinking. His book, *The Loss of the SS Titanic*, was the first published first-hand account of the tragedy.

Brothers whose father perished in the sinking

Third Class passengers were mostly immigrants moving from the UK to the US or to Canada.

A Third Class ticket on board the ship cost approximately £9, which would equate to about £754 today.

A Third Class child's ticket was £3, which is about £251 today.

There were many large families on board the ship with Third Class tickets, including the Sage family (nine children), the Andersson family (five children), the Goodwin family (six children).

The Goodwin family with five of their six children

Millvina Dean was the youngest passenger on board the Titanic, at the age of two months. She survived the sinking and was the last survivor to die in 2009.

CHAPTER 4: INTERIOR OF THE TITANIC

The first-class reception room aboard the Titanic

Titanic had a gymnasium, a swimming pool, libraries, and high-end restaurants.

Titanic's first-class gymnasium

There were also a squash court, a salt water swimming pool, electric baths, Turkish baths, a barbershop, elevators, promenades, and even kennels for dogs of the First Class passengers.

Titanic's reading and writing room

Titanic's First Class passengers enjoyed an opulent entrance to their dining room.

The Verandah Café and Palm Court were located on A Deck.

The Café Parisian was located on B Deck and attracted the younger First Class passengers during the daytime.

There were two Millionaire Suites on Titanic, which were located on either side of B Deck. Each suite had its own promenade. Suite B-52 was occupied by Bruce Ismay, Chairman and managing director of White Star Line, during the maiden voyage.

Titanic's Grand Staircase

Titanic's Second Class passengers had access to a library and the men could use a private smoking room.

The children of the Second Class passengers could read in the library or play shuffleboard on the Second Class promenade.

The Third Class passengers had their own dining facilities, which included chairs instead of benches, and their own kitchen staff.

The price of the Third Class ticket also included food during the voyage, which was different from other passenger liners.

Single passengers in the Third Class were separated according to sex. The single women were in the stern section of the ship, in cabins that held two to six individuals. The men were in the bow section of the ship, in cabins that held up to ten individuals.

The Third Class passengers also had their own common room, where they could play games such as chess or cards.

There were locked gates that prevented the classes from mingling amongst each other.

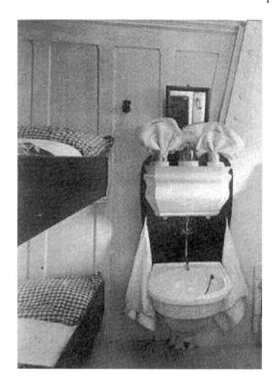

Third Class cabin

CHAPTER 5: MAIDEN VOYAGE OF THE TITANIC

Poster from 1912, advertising the RMS Titanic

The Titanic's radio call sign was "MGY".

Titanic's first and last voyage began on April 10, 1912 at about 6:00 a.m.

Thomas Andrews boarded the ship at about 6:00 a.m.

Captain Smith boarded the ship at about 7:30 a.m.

The crew performed a lifeboat drill at about 9:00 a.m. for 30 minutes.

The Second Class and Third Class passengers started to board the ship at about 10:15 a.m.

The First Class passengers started to board at about 11:30 a.m.

Titanic at the Southampton docks

Titanic cast off at approximately 12:00 noon or slightly after.

Leaving Southampton on April 10, 1912

Titanic anchored at Cherbourg Harbor at about 6:20 p.m. to pick up passengers, cargo, and mail.

Titanic set off for Queenstown, Ireland at about 10:00 p.m.

On April 11, 1912, Titanic arrived in Queenstown Harbor at about 12:00 noon.

Titanic departed Queenstown Harbor at about 2:00 p.m.

Titanic reached its official starting point of the trans-Atlantic crossing, Daunt's Rock, at about 2:20 p.m.

By about 1:20 p.m. on April 12, 1912, Titanic had travelled 484 miles since leaving Daunt's Rock, during the 1st day of its trans-Atlantic crossing.

By about 2:10 p.m. on April 13, 1912, Titanic had travelled an additional 519 miles, during the 2nd day of its trans-Atlantic crossing.

The ship's wireless communication stopped working at about 1:10 a.m. on April 14, 1912, but was fixed by about 8:00 a.m.

On April 14, 1912, Titanic received an ice warning at about 2:45 p.m.

By about 3:00 p.m. on April 14, 1912, Titanic had travelled an additional 546 miles, during the 3rd day of its trans-Atlantic crossing.

At about 11:40 p.m. on April 14, 1912, Titanic hit an iceberg.

At about 2:20 a.m. on April 15, 1912, Titanic sank.

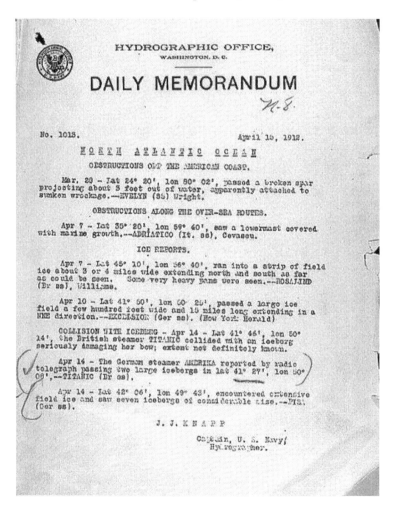

Memorandum issued by the US Navy on April 15, 1912

CHAPTER 6: SINKING OF THE TITANIC

New York newspaper, *The New York Herald,* front page
from April 15, 1912

The Titanic sank in the North Atlantic Ocean on
April 15, 1912 after hitting an iceberg.

When the Titanic sank, she was travelling from Southampton, UK to New York City, US.

Titanic hit the iceberg at approximately 11:40 p.m. on April 14, 1912 and sank 2 hours and 40 minutes later on April 15, 1912.

Titanic hit an iceberg approximately 600km (375 miles) south of Newfoundland, Canada.

Photo of the iceberg that Titanic probably hit, taken five days after the sinking by a Bohemian seaman

Almost two hours after the Titanic sank, the RMS Carpathia, a Cunard liner arrived.

The RMS Carpathia saved approximately 705 survivors of the sinking.

Italian newspaper, *Il secolo*, front page from April 17, 1912

More than 1,500 people died during the sinking of the Titanic.

Of the 711 souls who survived the sinking of the Titanic, one passenger died in a lifeboat during the night.

Of the 711 souls who survived the sinking, five died while on board the Carpathia and were buried at sea.

The Carpathia recovered 209 identified and unidentified victims of the sinking.

All 209 recovered victims were brought to Halifax, Nova Scotia, Canada, where 59 were repatriated, 121 were buried in the Fairview Lawn Cemetery (non-denominational), 19 were buried in the Mount Olivet Cemetery (Roman Catholic), and 10 were buried in the Jewish Baron de Hirsch Cemetery. The remaining bodies were either delivered to family members or buried at sea.

Lifeboats recovered from the Titanic were used by
other ships following the sinking

CHAPTER 7: SURVIVORS OF THE TITANIC

Lifeboat filled with survivors of the Titanic, taken by a passenger of the rescue ship, Carpathia

There were six First Class children aboard, and five survived.

There were 24 Second Class children aboard, and they all survived.

There were 79 Third Class children aboard, and 27 survived.

Of the 144 First Class women on board, 140 survived.

Of the 93 Second Class women on board, 80 survived.

Of the 165 Third Class women on board, 76 survived.

There were 175 First Class men on board, and 57 survived.

There were 168 Second Class men on board, and 14 survived.

There were 462 Third Class men on board, and 75 survived.

In total, 32% of Titanic's passengers survived the sinking.

Violet Jessop was a crew member aboard the Titanic who survived. She also survived the sinking of the Britannic and was aboard the Olympic when she was rammed in 1911.

CHAPTER 8: TITANIC MUSEUMS AND MEMORIALS

In Liverpool, at the ship's port of registry, there is a memorial to the 214 engineering crew members who died during the disaster.

Southampton, where many of the crew members originated, also has a memorial to the engineering crew of the Titanic.

In Northern Ireland, an attraction called Titanic Belfast opened on March 31, 2012. It was built at the shipyard where Titanic was built.

The company authorized to salvage the wreck, RMS Titanic Inc., has opened an exhibition called, Titanic, in Las Vegas, Nevada at the Luxor Hotel and Casino. It contains a 22-ton piece of the ship's hull. The company also runs a travelling museum called, Titanic: The Artifact Exhibition.

Halifax, Nova Scotia is home to the Maritime Museum of the Atlantic and displays the items that were found in the ocean during the first few days after the sinking.

The Titanic Museum Attraction has two locations. One is in Branson, Missouri and the other is in Pigeon Forge, Tennessee.

CHAPTER 9: MOVIES ABOUT THE TITANIC

SAVED FROM THE TITANIC

Saved from the Titanic was the first film about the sinking and was released just 29 days after the disaster. Silent film actress Dorothy Gibson starred in the film and was an actual survivor of the sinking.

The Director was Etienne Arnaud.

Actress Dorothy Gibson also wrote the movie.

The movie was released on May 14, 1912 in the US.

The black and white silent movie was 10 minutes long.

Theatrical poster for the 1912 release of Saved from the Titanic

A NIGHT TO REMEMBER

A Night to Remember was released in 1958 and is thought to be the most historically accurate film about the sinking.

The movie was directed by Roy Ward Baker and filmed in the UK.

Fourth Officer Joseph Boxhall was a technical advisor on the film.

Blueprints of the ship were used to create accurate sets.

The story was written by Walter Lord and the screenplay was written by Eric Ambler.

The film starred Kenneth More, Ronald Allen, Robert Ayres, Honor Blackman, Michael Goodliffe, and Laurence Naismith.

The movie premiered on July 1, 1958 in the UK.

The US premiere was on December 16, 1958.

The movie was 123 minutes in length and cost approximately $1,680,000 to produce.

Theatrical poster for the 1958 release of A Night to Remember

TITANIC

Titanic was released in 1997 and has been the most successful of all of the movies made about the Titanic.

The film was written and directed by James Cameron.

The film was 194 minutes in length.

The film was released on December 19, 1997.

The film starred Leonardo DiCaprio, Kate Winslet, Billy Zane, Kathy Bates, Frances Fisher, Gloria Stuart, Bill Paxton, Bernard Hill, David Warner, Victor Garber, Jonathan Hyde, and others.

The film was a fictionalized account of the sinking combined with a love story.

At the time it was made, Titanic was the most expensive film ever made, with a budget of approximately $200 million.

The film was nominated for 14 Academy Awards and won 11 of them, including Best Picture and Best Director.

Titanic was the first film to gross over $1 billion and was the highest-grossing film ever until 2010.

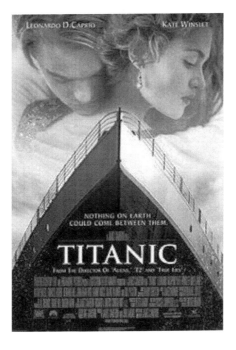

Theatrical poster for the 1997 release of *Titanic*

CHAPTER 10: LEGACY OF THE TITANIC

Following the sinking of the Titanic, the International Convention for the Safety of Life at Sea (SOLAS) was established in 1914. It remains in effect today with respect to maritime safety.

Blue Star Line announced on April 30, 2012 its plan to recreate the original ship in honour of the 100th anniversary of the sinking.

The ship will be called Titanic II.

The Titanic II will be just as luxurious as the original, but will have all modern amenities now available.

The first model testing of the proposed Titanic II was held in September, 2013.

The ship is scheduled to be launched in China in 2016.

Titanic II's maiden voyage will retrace the original voyage from Southampton to New York.

The remains of the original Titanic were discovered in 1985.

It was largely believed that the Titanic sank intact, until the wreckage was discovered.

There are two main pieces of the wreck. The two sections are about 0.6km (1/3 mile) apart.

The bow, despite deterioration, is quite recognizable.

The stern section was damaged during its descent and crash on the ocean floor.

There is an 8km x 4.8km (5 x 3 miles) debris field around the wreck.

The debris field contains hundreds of thousands of items, such as personal effects, machinery, furniture, utensils, and ship debris.

No human remains have been found, as they have decayed, or have been absorbed into the ocean.

Salvagers have recovered thousands of artifacts from the wreckage and have put these items on display.

Salvagers are unable to raise the wreckage as it is too fragile.

Before the wreckage was discovered, it was thought that the ship would be intact and undisturbed as it was not known that there were sea creatures that lived at that depth.

After the wreckage was discovered, the ship was found to be inhabited by a wide variety of 28 species, including anemones, crabs, shrimp, starfish, and rattail fish.

Undersea creatures have consumed all wooden material on the ship, with the exception of anything that was made of teak.

Metal-eating bacteria are covering most of the hull. It will eventually be completely devoured until the hull is gone.

It is estimated that the bacteria will destroy the ship by about 2030.

In 2001, an American couple were married inside a submersible that had landed on the bow of Titanic.

The grandson of one of the surviving crew members accompanied the couple on their trip and became the first relative of a crew member to visit the wreck.

In 2010, the first detailed map of the debris field was generated from two underwater vehicles that took sonar scans of the area.

On the 100th anniversary of the sinking, the wreck became a World Heritage Site. At that time, the wreck's discoverer announced his plan to preserve the wreck by painting the hull with an anti-fouling paint.

The bow of the remains of the Titanic

The Titanic lies approximately 3,784m (12,415') below the surface of the Atlantic Ocean.

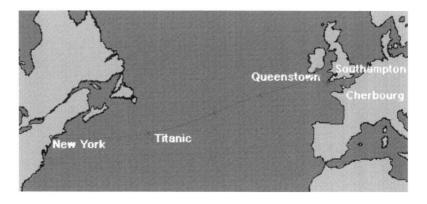

Map of approximate location of the remains of Titanic

CONCLUSION

Well, I hope you have enjoyed learning about the Titanic. I have always been fascinated with the great ship and I loved researching it while I was preparing to write this book.

The Titanic truly is one of the greatest tragedies in our history, one that will never be forgotten. This is obvious when you see that there are still movies being made about it, there are still monuments being erected to honor it, and those that are able are still trying to preserve it.

If you are like me, you now have the desire to see the movies again, or for the first time, if you haven't already seen them. I was happy to discover that the first silent film is available for viewing online. Just visit YouTube and type in "Surviving the Titanic."

Enjoy!

ENJOY THIS BOOK?

I see you've made it all the way to the end of my book. I'm so glad you enjoyed it enough to get all the way through! If you liked the book, would you be open to leaving me a 4 or 5 star review? You see, I'm a self-published author, and when people like you are able to give me reviews, it helps me out in a big way. You can leave a review for me at the Amazon page for this book (just click on the picture below).

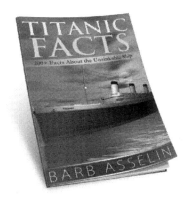

It'd really mean a lot to me.

Thank you.

Barb Asselin

Made in the USA
Lexington, KY
27 May 2014